DER STRUWWELPETER

MERRY
STORIES
AND FUNNY
PICTURES

HEINRICH HOFFMANN

Contents

DER STRUWWELPETER
MERRY STORIES AND FUNNY PICTURES
By Heinrich Hoffman

First published in German in 1845 as
Lustige Geschichten und drollige Bilder mit 15 schön kolorierten Tafeln
für Kinder von 3–6 Jahren

and in 1858 as
Der Struwwelpeter

This English edition 2014

Scrawny Goat Books
scrawnygoatbooks.com

ISBN 9781647646288

Merry Stories And Funny Pictures

When the children have been good,
That is, be it understood,
Good at meal-times, good at play,
Good all night and good all day—
They shall have the pretty things
Merry Christmas always brings.

Naughty, romping girls and boys
Tear their clothes and make a noise,
Spoil their pinafores and frocks,
And deserve no Christmas-box.
Such as these shall never look
At this pretty Picture-book.

Shock-headed Peter

Just look at him!
there he stands,
With his nasty hair and hands.
See! his nails are never cut;
They are grimed as black as soot;
And the sloven, I declare,
Never once has combed his hair;
Anything to me is sweeter
Than to see Shock-headed Peter.

Cruel Frederick

Here is cruel Frederick, see!
A horrid wicked boy was he;
He caught the flies, poor little things,
And then tore off their tiny wings,
He killed the birds, and broke the
chairs,
And threw the kitten down the stairs;
And oh! far worse than all beside,
He whipped his Mary, till she cried.

The trough was full, and faithful Tray
Came out to drink one sultry day;
He wagged his tail, and wet his lip,
When cruel Fred snatched up a whip,
And whipped poor Tray till he was sore,
And kicked and whipped him more and more:
At this, good Tray grew very red,
And growled, and bit him till he bled;
Then you should only have been by,
To see how Fred did scream and cry!

So Frederick had to go to bed:
His leg was very sore and red!
The Doctor came, and shook his head,
And made a very great to-do,
And gave him nasty physic too.

But good dog Tray is happy now;
He has no time to say "Bow-wow!"
He seats himself in Frederick's chair
And laughs to see the nice things there:
The soup he swallows, sup by sup—
And eats the pies and puddings up.

The Dreadful Story of Harriet and the Matches

It almost makes me cry to tell
What foolish Harriet befell.
Mamma and Nurse went out one day
And left her all alone at play.
Now, on the table close at hand,
A box of matches chanced to stand;
And kind Mamma and Nurse had told her,
That, if she touched them, they would scold
her.
But Harriet said: "Oh, what a pity!
For, when they burn, it is so pretty;
They crackle so, and spit, and flame;
Mamma, too, often does the same."

The pussy-cats heard this,
And they began to hiss,
And stretch their claws,
And raise their paws;
"Me-ow," they said, "me-ow, me-o,
You'll burn to death, if you do so."

But Harriet would not take advice:
She lit a match, it was so nice!
It crackled so, it burned so clear—
Exactly like the picture here.
She jumped for joy and ran about
And was too pleased to put it out.

The Pussy-cats saw this,
And said: "Oh, naughty, naughty Miss!"
And stretched their claws,
And raised their paws:
"'Tis very, very wrong, you know,
Me-ow, me-o, me-ow, me-o,
You will be burnt, if you do so."

And see! oh, what dreadful thing!
The fire has caught her apron-string;
Her apron burns, her arms, her hair—
　　　She burns all over everywhere.

Then how the pussy-cats did mew—
What else, poor pussies, could they do?
They screamed for help, 'twas all in vain!
So then they said: "We'll scream again;
Make haste, make haste, me-ow, me-o,
　　　She'll burn to death; we told her so."

So she was burnt, with all her clothes,
And arms, and hands, and eyes, and nose;
　　　Till she had nothing more to lose
　　　Except her little scarlet shoes;
And nothing else but these was found
　　　Among her ashes on the ground.

And when the good cats sat beside
The smoking ashes, how they cried!
"Me-ow, me-oo, me-ow, me-oo,
What will Mamma and Nursey do?"
Their tears ran down their cheeks so fast,
　　　They made a little pond at last.

7

As he had often done before,
The woolly-headed Black-a-moor
One nice fine summer's day went out
To see the shops, and walk about;
And, as he found it hot, poor fellow,
He took with him his green umbrella,
Then Edward, little noisy wag,
Ran out and laughed, and waved his flag;
And William came in jacket trim,
And brought his wooden hoop with him;
And Arthur, too, snatched up his toys
And joined the other naughty boys.
So, one and all set up a roar,
And laughed and hooted more and more,
And kept on singing,—only think!—
"Oh, Blacky, you're as black as ink!"

Now tall Agrippa lived close by—
So tall, he almost touched the sky;
He had a mighty inkstand, too,
In which a great goose-feather grew;
He called out in an angry tone
"Boys, leave the Black-a-moor alone!
For, if he tries with all his might,
He cannot change from black to white."
But, ah! they did not mind a bit
What great Agrippa said of it;
But went on laughing, as before,
And hooting at the Black-a-moor.

Then great Agrippa foams with rage—
Look at him on this very page!
He seizes Arthur, seizes Ned,
Takes William by his little head;

And they may scream and kick and call
Into the ink he dips them all
Into the inkstand, one, two, three
Till they are black as black can be
Turn the page, and you shall see

10

There they are, and there they run!
The Black-a-moor enjoys the fun.
They have been made as black as crows,
Quite black all over, eyes and nose,
And legs, and arms, and heads, and toes,
And trousers, pinafores, and toys—
The silly little inky boys!
Because they set up such a roar,
And teased the harmless Black-a-moor.

The Story of the Man that went out Shooting

This is the man that shoots the hares;
This is the coat he always wears:
With game-bag, powder-horn, and gun
He's going out to have some fun.

He finds it hard, without a pair
Of spectacles, to shoot the hare.

The hare sits snug in leaves and grass
And laughs to see the green man pass.

Now, as the sun grew very hot,
And he a heavy gun had got,
He lay down underneath a tree
And went to sleep, as you may see.
And, while he slept like any top,
The little hare came, hop, hop, hop,
Took gun and spectacles, and then
On her hind legs went off again.

The green man wakes and sees her place
The spectacles upon her face;
And now she's trying all she can
To shoot the sleepy, green-coat man.
He cries and screams and runs away;
The hare runs after him all day
And hears him call out everywhere:
"Help! Fire! Help! The Hare! The Hare!"

At last he stumbled at the well,
Head over ears, and in he fell.
The hare stopped short, took aim and, hark!
Bang went the gun—she missed her mark!

The poor man's wife was drinking up
Her coffee in her coffee-cup;
The gun shot cup and saucer through;
"Oh dear!" cried she; "what shall I do?"
There lived close by the cottage there
The hare's own child, the little hare;
And while she stood upon her toes,
The coffee fell and burned her nose.
"Oh dear!" she cried, with spoon in hand,
"Such fun I do not understand."

The Story of Little Suck-a-Thumb

One day Mamma said "Conrad dear,
I must go out and leave you here.
But mind now, Conrad, what I say,
Don't suck your thumb while I'm away.
The great tall tailor always comes
To little boys who suck their thumbs;
And ere they dream what he's about,
He takes his great sharp scissors out,
And cuts their thumbs clean off—and then,
You know, they never grow again."

Mamma had scarcely turned her back,
The thumb was in, Alack! Alack!

The door flew open, in he ran,
The great, long, red-legged scissor-man.
Oh! children, see! the tailor's come
And caught out little Suck-a-Thumb.
Snip! Snap! Snip! the scissors go;
And Conrad cries out "Oh! Oh! Oh!"
Snip! Snap! Snip! They go so fast,
That both his thumbs are off at last.

Mamma comes home: there Conrad stands,
And looks quite sad, and shows his hands;
"Ah!" said Mamma, "I knew he'd come
To naughty little Suck-a-Thumb."

The Story of Augustus,
who would not have any Soup

Augustus was a chubby lad
Fat ruddy cheeks Augustus had
And everybody saw with joy
The plump and hearty, healthy boy
He ate and drank as he was told
And never let his soup get cold
But one day, one cold winter's day
He screamed out "Take the soup away
O take the nasty soup away
I won't have any soup today."

Next day, now look, the picture shows
How lank and lean Augustus grows
Yet, though he feels so weak and ill
The naughty fellow cries out stil
"Not any soup for me, I say
O take the nasty soup away
I won't have any soup today."

The third day comes: Oh what a sin
To make himself so pale and thin.
Yet, when the soup is put on table,
He screams, as loud as he is able,
"Not any soup for me, I say
O take the nasty soup away
I WON'T have any soup today."

Look at him, now the fourth day's come
He scarcely weighs a sugar-plum;
He's like a little bit of thread,
And, on the fifth day, he was—dead

The Story of Fidgety Philip

"Let me see if Philip can
Be a little gentleman;
Let me see if he is able
To sit still for once at table":
Thus Papa bade Phil behave;
And Mamma looked very grave.
But fidgety Phil,
He won't sit still;
He wriggles,
And giggles,
And then, I declare,
Swings backwards and forwards,
And tilts up his chair,
Just like any rocking horse—
"Philip! I am getting cross!"

See the naughty, restless child
Growing still more rude and wild,
Till his chair falls over quite.
Philip screams with all his might,
Catches at the cloth, but then
That makes matters worse again.
Down upon the ground they fall,
Glasses, plates, knives, forks, and all.
How Mamma did fret and frown,
When she saw them tumbling down!
And Papa made such a face!
Philip is in sad disgrace.

Where is Philip, where is he?
Fairly covered up you see!
Cloth and all are lying on him;
He has pulled down all upon him.
What a terrible to-do!
Dishes, glasses, snapt in two!
Here a knife, and there a fork!
Philip, this is cruel work.
Table all so bare, and ah!
Poor Papa, and poor Mamma
Look quite cross, and wonder how
They shall have their dinner now.

The Story of Johnny Head-in-Air

As he trudged along to school,
It was always Johnny's rule
To be looking at the sky
And the clouds that floated by;
But what just before him lay,
In his way,
Johnny never thought about;
So that every one cried out
"Look at little Johnny there,
Little Johnny Head-In-Air!"

Running just in Johnny's way
Came a little dog one day;
Johnny's eyes were still astray
Up on high,
In the sky;
And he never heard them cry
"Johnny, mind, the dog is nigh!"
Bump!
Dump!
Down they fell, with such a thump,
Dog and Johnny in a lump!

Once, with head as high as ever,
Johnny walked beside the river.
Johnny watched the swallows trying
Which was cleverest at flying.
Oh! what fun!
Johnny watched the bright round sun
Going in and coming out;
This was all he thought about.
So he strode on, only think!
To the river's very brink,
Where the bank was high and steep,
And the water very deep;
And the fishes, in a row,
Stared to see him coming so.

One step more! oh! sad to tell!
Headlong in poor Johnny fell.
And the fishes, in dismay,
Wagged their tails and swam away.

There lay Johnny on his face
With his nice red writing-case
But, as they were passing by
Two strong men had heard him cry
And, with sticks, these two strong men
Hooked poor Johnny out again

Oh! you should have seen him shiver
When they pulled him from the river.
He was in a sorry plight!
Dripping wet, and such a fright!
Wet all over, everywhere,
Clothes, and arms, and face, and hair:
Johnny never will forget
What it is to be so wet.

And the fishes, one, two, three,
Are come back again, you see;
Up they came the moment after,
To enjoy the fun and laughter.
Each popped out his little head,
And, to tease poor Johnny, said
"Silly little Johnny, look,
You have lost your writing-book!"

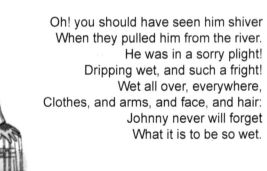

The Story of Flying Robert

When the rain comes tumbling down
In the country or the town,
All good little girls and boys
Stay at home and mind their toys.
Robert thought, "No, when it pours,
It is better out of doors."
Rain it did, and in a minute
Bob was in it.
Here you see him, silly fellow,
Underneath his red umbrella.

What a wind! oh! how it whistles
Through the trees and flowers and thistles!
It has caught his red umbrella:
Now look at him, silly fellow—
Up he flies
To the skies.
No one heard his screams and cries;
Through the clouds the rude wind bore
him,
And his hat flew on before him.

Soon they got to such a height,
They were nearly out of sight.
And the hat went up so high,
That it nearly touched the sky.
No one ever yet could tell
Where they stopped, or where they fell:
Only this one thing is plain,
Bob was never seen again!

If you enjoyed The Straw-Headed Peter, you will LOVE

Max und Moritz: A Boy's Tale in Seven Tricks

by Wilhelm Busch

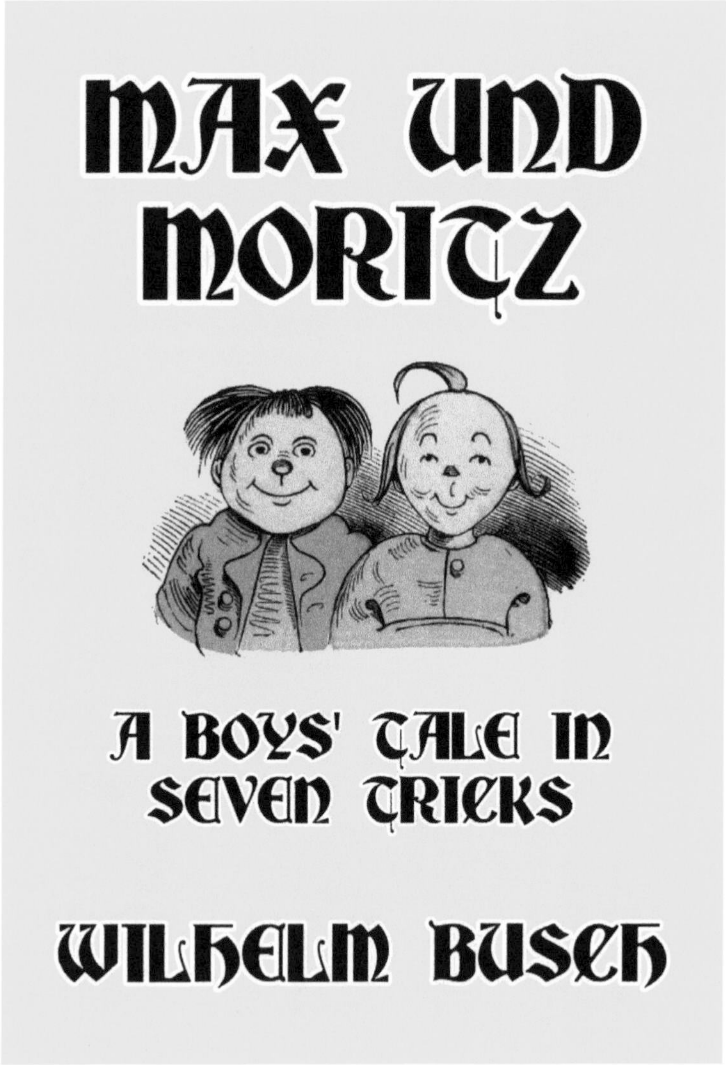
MAX UND MORITZ
A BOYS' TALE IN SEVEN TRICKS
WILHELM BUSCH

Also available from Scrawny Goat Publishing

CPSIA information can be obtained
at www.ICGtesting.com
Printed in the USA
BVHW022141220721
612706BV00003B/13

9 781647 646288